Memorial Book Shelf

of the

Franklin Library

Presented In Memory Of
MARIE MAYS

By

BILL & BARBARA HART

1994

Responsible Pet Care

Cats

Responsible Pet Care

Cats

PAM JAMESON

Rourke Publications, Inc.
Vero Beach, FL 32964

© 1989 Rourke Publications, Inc.

All rights reserved. No part of this book may be reproduced or utilized in any form or by any means, electronic or mechanical including photocopying, recording or by any information storage and retrieval system without permission in writing from the publisher.

Library of Congress Cataloging-in-Publication Data

Jameson, Pam, 1942-
   Cats/by Pam Jameson.
     p. cm - (Responsible pet care)
   Includes index.
   Summary: Describes the different varieties of cats and discusses how to care for them as pets.
   ISBN 0-86625-183-9
   1. Cats - Juvenile literature. [1. Cats.] I. Title. II. Series.
SF445.7.J35 1989
636.8-dc19   88-39974
                    CIP
                    AC

CONTENTS

1	Why Choose A Cat?	6
2	Varieties	8
3	Buying A Kitten	10
4	Visiting The Veterinarian	12
5	Your Cat And Other Pets	14
6	Keeping Your Cat Safe	15
7	Early Training	16
8	Feeding	19
9	Grooming And Claw Care	22
10	Travel	25
11	Ailments	27
12	Health And Longevity	29
	Glossary	30
	Index	31

Why Choose A Cat?

Of all the small companion animals, tiny kittens are perhaps the most appealing. As soon as they can stumble and crawl from the side of the mother cat they are ready to explore the world around them and to make friends with the human race. They will play with anything from a passing feather to their own tail, and when they are tired, all they want is a soft warm place to sleep. Their owner's lap is a perfect spot. As it grows up, every kitten develops a distinct personality and starts to live in that rather secret world of cats. Every cat wants independence, but its own home and its first owner will always be something special.

Cats can be the ideal pet for almost anyone. They can live happily in the country or in a city apartment. They can fit in as part of a large noisy family or live quietly as the sole companion of an elderly person. Cats have very clean habits, make little noise, and do not cost much to feed.

Cats are independent creatures. This male tabby is out on the prowl.

Cats come in many different colors and coat textures.

Unlike dogs, which come in all shapes and sizes, you can be quite sure that your little kitten will not grow into a huge animal that outeats the rest of the family members combined. You can choose from a range of breeds with different characteristics, coat textures, and colors. You can buy an expensive cat or get one for free.

But before you decide that a cat is the right pet for you, think again: Will you make a good cat owner?

The first thing to remember is that your tiny kitten will need to be taken care of for many years. Many cats live for fifteen years or more. For all of that lifetime it will be your responsibility to provide regular meals, a comfortable place to sleep, and veterinary treatment when it is needed. You will have to make sure that you can pay for **inoculations** and **neutering** or perhaps be prepared to look after one or more litters of kittens. And when you go on vacation you will have to make sure that your cat is being well cared for.

If you are willing to do these things as well as you can — and with loving care — you will make a good cat owner.

Varieties

Cats can be divided into two main types: long-haired and short-haired. Each group contains many different breeds, and some cats can be a mixture of more than one. The best way to see the enormous variety of purebred cats is to go to a show where breeders put their cats on display. Cat lovers are always happy to talk about their animals, and you can learn a lot by looking and listening as you go around the cat pens.

A **pedigreed** cat can cost a lot of money, but sometimes breeders will have a kitten that is not quite good enough for showing. Perhaps its tail is slightly too long, or its ears are at the wrong angle, or its color is not just right. None of these flaws will make any difference to its health or temperament. You can get a very good kitten inexpensively this way, but you will probably not be given the pedigree papers that go along with it.

Humane societies are full of older cats that need new and loving owners.

You can see many pedigree cats like this Chinchilla and her kittens at cat shows.

    Many people get their cats from friends or neighbors who are looking for homes for kittens. Kittens are also advertised in most newspapers. Pet shops often have a good selection of kittens, and humane societies are full of older cats who need a new and loving owner. The local veterinarian may even have a client who has kittens for sale. You will have no difficulty in finding a kitten or a cat: your greatest problem will be choosing which one to take.

    Tiny kittens are so appealing that your first impulse might be to choose one over a grown-up cat. If there is no one home all day, though, a kitten could be very lonely. Like all young babies, it has to be fed at frequent intervals. An older cat, on the other hand, would very soon adapt its ways to your home and would not mind so much being left alone for part of the day. Whether you decide on a kitten or a cat, make sure you get one that is healthy.

Buying A Kitten

A mother cat will feed her kittens with her own milk until they are about three weeks old. Even when they start to eat on their own they will still need their mother's milk until they are around six weeks old. If they can be left with the mother until they are seven or eight weeks old, she will teach them to use a litter box and to groom and wash themselves. Kittens taken away from their mother at too early an age often have behavior problems when they grow older.

A healthy kitten should be very active with a soft, shiny coat and bright eyes that are clear and not watery. Kittens get their first set of teeth at about 6 weeks, so a look inside the mouth can confirm a kitten's age. The ears should be clean and pink inside with no brown crust or unpleasant smell. The body should feel firm with the ribs and backbone well covered. A distended belly is not

These kittens are four days old. Their ginger mother is rather unusual. Most ginger cats are male, and the three ginger kittens are all males.

a good sign. If you can see the whole litter, watch them at play for a few minutes. Avoid the timid one who hides in a corner – he probably needs to be left with his mother for a bit longer. Pedigreed kittens should be registered with either the CFA (Cat Fanciers Association) or ACFA (American Cat Fanciers Association). If for any reason the registration is not available, the kitten must be sold as unregistered.

Ask the breeder or owner of the kittens if the litter has been **wormed** and if so, the date when this was done. Find out what the kittens have been fed and try to keep to the same diet formula for at least a week.

Male and female cats make equally good pets, so it does not really matter which you choose. You may even want two kittens. In this case you should choose either two females or a male and a female. Two male cats do not always get along well together.

Two kittens together are always fun. Choose two sisters or a male and female from the same litter.

Visiting The Veterinarian

As soon as possible, take your kitten or kittens to your veterinarian. If your kitten has a pedigree take that along with you. Your veterinarian will check your pet thoroughly and advise you about the inoculations needed to protect your kitten from infectious cat diseases. He or she may ask you to hold your kitten while it receives a shot and explain about having your cat neutered. This simple operation, performed at around five months, will prevent your female from giving birth to unwanted litters and your male cat from straying from home and getting involved in street fights.

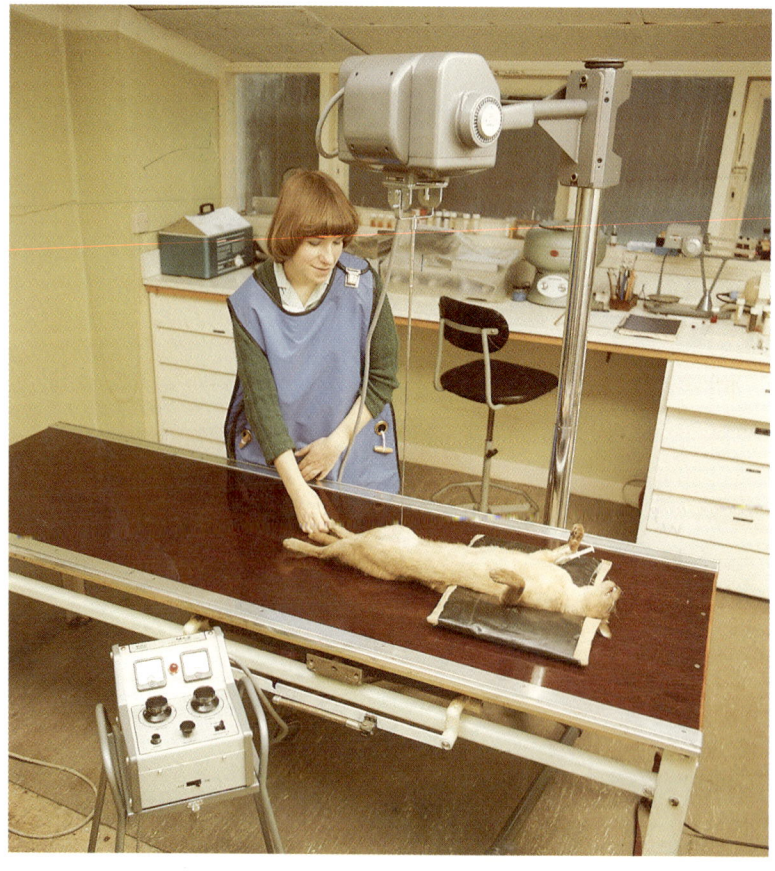

Veterinarians have well equipped clinics. The veterinary nurse is preparing a patient for X-ray.

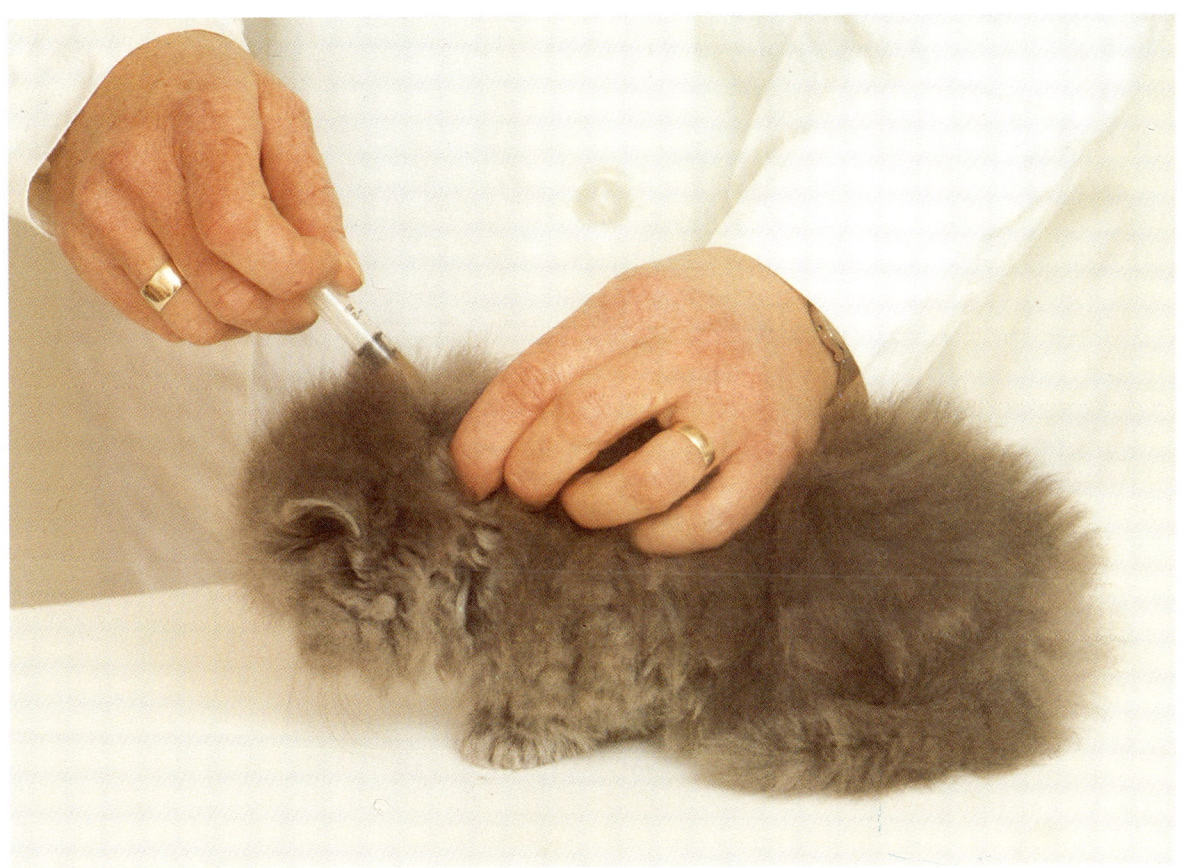

Kittens must have shots against some infectious diseases.

Some people continue to believe that a female cat must have at least one litter for her own good. This is not true. Female cats that have been neutered before giving birth are perfectly happy and healthy. Sadly, there are far too many kittens born every year. You should not breed your cat unless you can be very sure that you will find good and loving homes for all the kittens.

If, however, you have taken in a cat that is already pregnant, you must look after her and give her extra food while she is carrying her kittens. Cats are pregnant for about nine weeks. As the time of the birth draws near, most cats have their kittens without any help from humans and often resent human interference. Let her have a nice quiet place and be near in case she needs help. Phone your veterinarian if you are worried that everything is not going well. Handle the kittens as little as possible and start looking for homes for them right away. You may even wish to keep one for yourself.

Your Cat And Other Pets

If you have other pets at home, how will they react to the new arrival? An older cat may spit and hiss at a newcomer. Try not to leave them alone together for the first few days. Instead, stick around to protect the new one or soothe the older one. Never try to force them together. Cats are very individual, and some cats will always prefer to be aloof. Provide plenty of feeding dishes and an extra litter pan. In time the newcomer will be at least tolerated, if not exactly made welcome.

If you already have a dog, stay around while the two animals are getting to know each other. Most dogs love to play with kittens, but their games may be just a bit too rough for a young kitten.

If you have birds or small pets such as hamsters, gerbils, or mice, put their cages well out of harm's way. Remember, cats are very curious, and they can climb. Cover aquariums and fish bowls to prevent accidents or illegal fishing.

The owner should stay nearby while the kittens and the collie make friends, just in case play gets a little too rough.

Keeping Your Cat Safe

If you have a garden, do not let the cat out alone until it is used to you and the new surroundings. Then let it out for short periods of time and stay outside with it. Soon you will be able to let it in and out on its own.

Look around your home and make it safe. Don't leave upstairs windows open, and if you have a balcony be sure that the cat cannot climb over or squeeze through the railings. It is a myth that cats can fall from any height and land without injury. Every year hundreds of cats have to be treated for broken bones.

If you live near a busy road or in an apartment, you may decide to keep your cat inside. Cats have very little traffic sense, and many are killed and injured by cars, especially at night when they are dazzled and confused by headlights. Remember that cats do not need long walks or outdoor exercise to keep fit. They can be kept happily in a limited space, provided they are given lots of opportunities to climb and hide. A cardboard carton with holes for doors and windows will keep a kitten amused for hours.

Cats love to climb, but every year hundreds of cats are treated for broken bones. Tree climbing should be discouraged.

Early Training

Cats are full of curiosity, and your new pet will soon want to explore every inch of your home, including the tops of furniture. For the first few weeks, put all breakable or precious ornaments in a safe place.

Young kittens need plenty of rest and sleep, so restrain your impulse to pick up your new kitten and play with it too often. If the weather is cold, fix up a soft bed with a hot water bottle under a blanket. When it wakes up, take it to the litter box. If a mistake is made, do not punish or scold the kitten, but gently and firmly show it how to scratch in the litter. Be full of praise when it gets the right idea. It won't take long, as cats are naturally very clean animals. Kittens who have remained with their mother for eight weeks will already be trained to use the litter box.

Place the litter box in a quiet part of the house but never just next to the feeding station. Make sure that the box is cleaned out every day. Some boxes come with a cover, which gives the cat privacy and also hides the litter box from view. Many cat litters contain deodorant to prevent the box from smelling bad. Place a newspaper on the floor under the pan to catch litter scratched out by accident.

Young kittens need plenty of rest and sleep.

Kittens are naturally clean and will quickly learn to use a litter tray.

Bad habits can be learned just as easily as good ones. Do not let your cat get away with antisocial behavior. If it begins to scratch the furniture, call its name and say "No". You will use its name often, so give it a simple name. Cats will learn to recognize their name and are also very sensitive to your tone of voice. You too will soon learn what your cat wants by the different sounds it makes.

Persistent bad behavior can be stopped by spraying your cat with water, either from a squirt gun or a plant sprayer. This technique works well because your cat doesn't associate the punishment with you, only with the behavior that brings it on.

Many cat toys contain the herb catnip. Few young kittens pay attention to this but most mature cats seem to get great enjoyment from sniffing and rolling on catnip.

A Shopping List For Your New Cat

Food and water dishes
Litter pan (one with low sides for a kitten)
Cat litter and scoop
Cat collar with bell
A scratching post
A carrying case or travel kennel
For long-haired cats — a soft grooming brush and a wire comb with widely spaced teeth

This handsome Persian cat likes its own sleeping basket with blankets and a hot water bottle in cold weather.

Feeding

Cats are **carnivores**, or meat eaters. Cats need a diet that is rich in protein and animal fat. They know this instinctively, and even a well fed cat will hunt for birds and small rodents if it has the opportunity.

Cats seldom overeat, and indeed some become very fussy and will decide to eat one kind of food only, refusing everything else. Some cats develop a craving for liver or fish, but this can lead to a badly balanced diet. It is most important to train your cat to eat a wide variety of cat food. A complete food contains a balanced mixture of proteins, carbohydrates, fats, vitamins, and minerals.

Water: Water is an essential part of a cat's diet. Always have a dish of clean water where your cat can reach it, but do not be surprised if your cat prefers water from a dripping faucet or a garden puddle.

Canned food: Food labeled "incomplete" should never be fed as a sole diet, even if your cat prefers it to other brands. Good quality canned food will cost more, but it will supply a complete diet. Always read what is on the label.

Even a well fed cat will go hunting for birds.

Dry food: Most stores offer a great variety of dried cat food. Most cats like the crunchy texture and the taste, and dry food is good for their teeth and gums. Make sure that fresh water is always available when your cat has dried food.

Semi-moist or moist foods: These are very convenient since they do not dry up and smell the way leftover canned food can do. The lack of odor means that they are not so tempting to some cats, but they make a useful substitute and are particularly good if you are traveling.

Cats prefer to eat a little at a time. Left in the wild state, they would eat only small animals or birds, so think of mouse-sized portions. Kittens should be fed three or four times a day; adult cats twice. Quantities depend on the age and size of the cat. A good guide is to feed kittens one large soupspoonful of food at each meal, gradually increasing this amount if it is all eaten.

Cats are carnivores, or meat eaters. Small rodents like mice are their natural prey.

Good quality canned food may cost a little more. Always read the label to make sure it is a nutritionally complete food.

Food should be given at room temperature and not taken straight out of the refrigerator. When eating, cats often pull food out of their dish, so a newspaper or mat under the bowls will help to make life easier for the housekeeper. Treats and leftover table food should be given only as a special reward and not as part of the diet.

Many cats cannot digest cow's milk and develop diarrhea from drinking it. Your pet shop or veterinarian can supply you with a milk substitute in powder form. This can be mixed with water to make a formula suitable for even the youngest kittens.

If you have a dog, you may find that the cat likes to eat its food. Even if the dog does not object, you should try to prevent this, since dog food does not supply nearly enough protein or fat to keep your cat healthy. A little now and then will do no harm, as long as the cat eats its own food as well. If you are feeding your cat chicken or fish as a special treat, be very careful to remove all the bones, including the tiny ones.

Grooming And Claw Care

Cats spend a lot of time washing and grooming themselves, using their tongues and paws. Long haired cats, however, cannot keep their coats in good order without some help. Even short haired varieties benefit from being brushed. Matts and tufts of fur can gather behind the ears, under the chin, between the legs, and under the tail. If these are allowed to form into solid lumps, they will cause a great deal of discomfort. In the worst cases, they can only be removed by the veterinarian who must give the cat an **anesthetic** and shear off the coat.

You can avoid this problem by grooming your cat daily. Some cats resent being brushed and combed, so you must be patient and reward your cat for good behavior. Talk to your cat as you groom it and keep each grooming session short. A little time spent every day is better than an hour once a week. While you are grooming you can check that your cat has no skin trouble or wounds.

A short haired cat can keep clean just by using tongue and paws, but combing will help to remove dead hair.

Long haired breeds need more help. A little time spent every day will keep your pet free of matts and tangles.

Cats shed hair all the time. If you have dark clothes and a light colored cat, you will soon see this yourself. Often a cat will swallow some of the hair it sheds. This hair forms into a furball in the stomach. Cats usually get rid of these by vomiting them up or passing them in the litter box.

Most cats get fleas at some time in their life. You may not be able to see them, but if the cat has been scratching frequently, look out for small black specks next to the skin. This is flea dirt and a sure sign that your cat has – or has had – fleas. In order to get rid of these pests, you must treat the cat and its surroundings. Pet supply stores sell powders that have been created especially for cats. Certain powders must not be used on young kittens. You must also buy a spray to kill any fleas that might be living in the carpet, couch, or other places at home. To prevent fleas on an adult cat, put a flea collar on it. Never use a flea collar on a sick cat, and consult a veterinarian before using one on young kittens. Some cats suffer from flea allergy and develop sores that will require treatment.

Cats' claws grow all the time, and cats normally keep their claws sharp by clawing at trees or scratching posts. If a cat is inactive, its claws will become very long and often catch on clothes and other items. The pet shop, grooming parlor, or veterinarian will cut your cat's claws. After you have been shown how to do it, you may be able to keep them trimmed yourself. It is a fairly simple job, but success depends on how co-operative your cat is.

Cats' claws grow all the time. This cat is making good use of a scratching block. Always check your cat for overgrown claws.

Travel

Even if you only intend to travel to the veterinarian and back, you will need a cat carrier. A cardboard one is fine for a very young kitten, but an older cat needs something stronger. Inexpensive molded plastic carriers are available at pet stores and are often advertised at discount stores. A zip-up bag can be used in an emergency, but be careful to zip it up far enough so the cat stays inside – cats can escape through a very tiny space.

If you are going on a long journey, you may have to feed your cat on the way. For trips of less than twelve hours, don't give your cat any food. Make sure that the cat has plenty of air, and don't leave the carrier in the sun. Take some water and a dish with you. Some cats are quite happy to travel as long as they can see their owner, so a carrier with a wire front is a good idea.

Cats often feel happier if they can see their owners while traveling. This secure wire carrier is a good idea.

If you know your cat gets nervous when traveling, ask your veterinarian to provide a **tranquilizer**, a pill to calm it down. *Never give your cat medicine intended for humans.* Some medicines that are good for humans are poisonous to cats. Do not try to hold your cat on your lap if you are traveling by car. For safety, keep your cat in its carrier whenever the car is moving.

If your family is going on a trip and you must leave your cat at home, make arrangements for a friend or neighbor to feed your cat every day. Cats can be left alone several days with ample food and water, but they get lonely.

If your family is going to be gone for a long time, you should arrange to leave your cat in a boarding kennel. Ask your veterinarian to recommend a suitable place; some veterinarians supply this service.

This tabby kitten will be quite safe on a car trip in this wicker basket, even without its mother. Don't forget to bring along food and water if the journey is to be longer than a few hours.

Ailments

Several signs point to a sick cat: loss of appetite, vomiting, runny eyes and nose, and diarrhea, for starters. A sick cat or one that is in pain will want to lie still and not be disturbed. It may look for a dark hiding place and refuse to come out, even for food. If this behavior persists for forty-eight hours, take the cat to the veterinarian. Modern medicine can cut short many illnesses, and you may find that as your cat recovers you will be able to go on with the treatment at home.

Good nursing is important, but cats do not make good patients. Put the invalid in a quiet place and the litter box within easy reach. Make a bed out of clean blankets, and be sure your cat is warm and out of drafts. If it does not want to eat, now is the time to offer that favorite food. Tempt its appetite with small portions, and if necessary, hand feed it for a day or so. Liquids are very important, and you should give your sick cat a little water from a spoon if it refuses to drink on its own.

Sick cats require special attention. Keep an invalid cat in a quiet, warm place out of drafts.

Cats can be very stubborn about taking pills or liquids that they don't like. A pill disguised in a piece of meat or some butter will soon be detected. By wrapping the cat in a blanket so that just its head is out, you may be able to get a pill right into its mouth. This method usually takes two people, and the cat will probably not let you do it a second time. If you crush the tablet well and mix it in yeast or meat extract, you can smear it on the cat's paws and it will be quickly licked off. Liquid medicine is slightly easier to give. Use a dropper or syringe to get it into the gap just behind the long upper front teeth and then tilt the head back. The cat will be forced to swallow the liquid. Here again you will probably need the assistance of someone to hold the cat in a blanket so you won't be scratched.

Cats can be very stubborn about taking their medicine. Getting a pill into the patient takes skill.

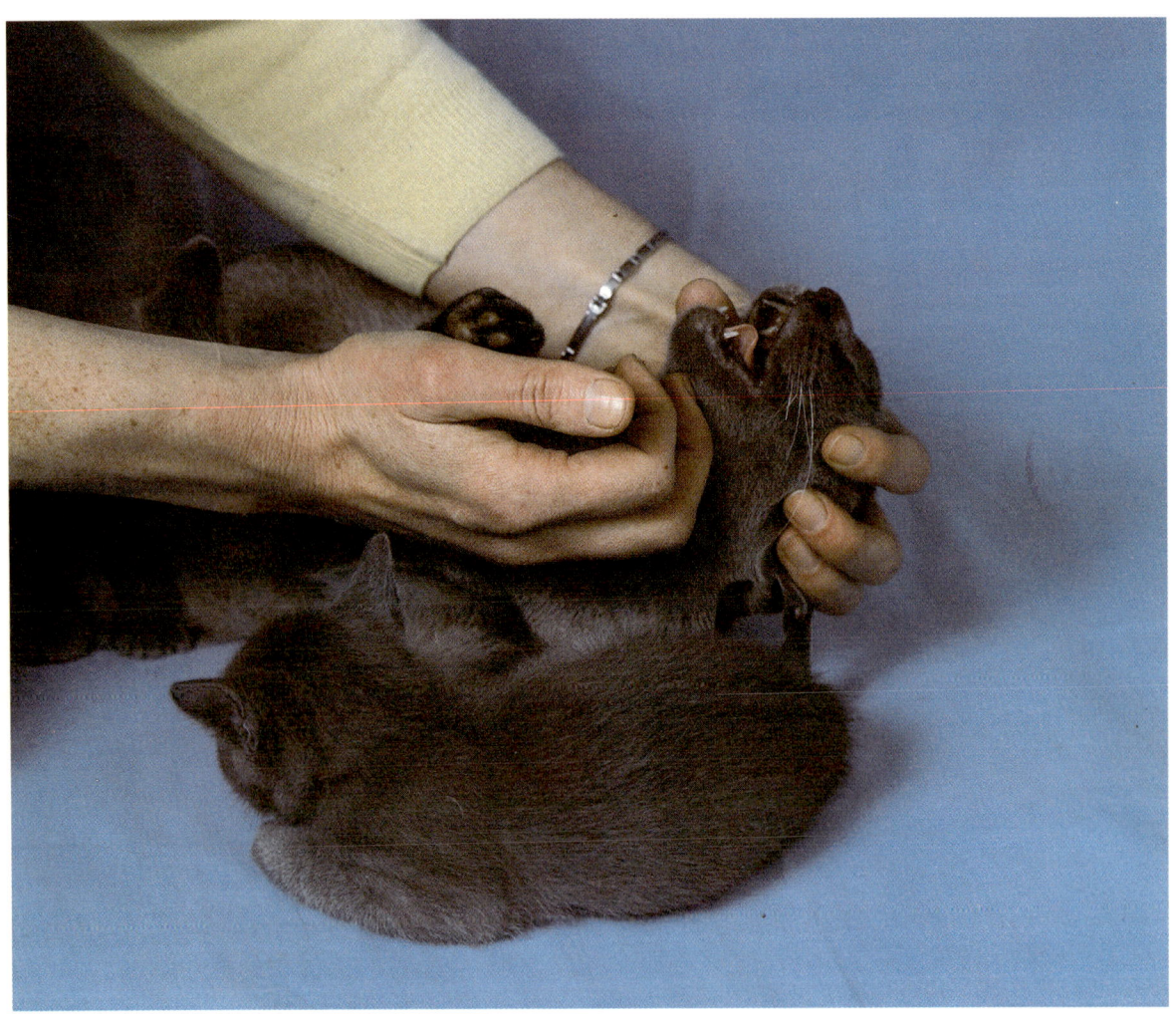

Health And Longevity

Cats grow old gracefully, and even very elderly cats will still play as they did when they were kittens. But gradually they will slow down and sleep for a great deal of the time. The soft shiny coat may get dull and even change color. The old cat has often lost some of its teeth and has difficulty eating. Old cats are more likely to suffer from disease, and many become thin although they are still well fed.

At some point, you may be faced with a difficult decision. If your cat is suffering, you must allow the veterinarian to give it an anesthetic to let it fall asleep gently and painlessly one last time. You can be with your cat right to the end. As a responsible cat owner, it is the least and last thing you can do for your friend.

This elderly gentleman has lost some teeth, and his coat no longer shines. He is slowing down and sleeps much of the time.

GLOSSARY

Anesthetic — A drug that is given to people or animals so that they lose their sense of feeling.

Carnivore — An animal that only eats meat.

Inoculations — Injections of substances that help prevent disease by building up a resistance to it.

Neutering — Performing a minor operation to ensure that an animal will not have babies.

Pedigree — A recorded history of parents and grandparents that proves a pure breeding.

Tranquilizer — A pill that calms down a person or animal.

Wormed — Relieved of any worms that sometimes are found inside an animal.

INDEX

American Cat Fanciers
    Association (ACFA)   11
Anesthetics   22, 29

Beds   16, 17
Boarding kennels   26
Breeds   7, 8

Cat carriers   18, 25
Cat Fanciers Association (CFA)   11
Catnip   17
Claws   24
Coat   10, 22, 29

Diarrhea   21, 27
Diet   11, 19, 21
Dogs   7, 14, 21

Ears   8, 10
Exercise   15
Eyes   10, 27

Falls   15
Feeding   19-21, 25, 27
Female cats   11, 12, 13
Fleas   24
Furballs   23

Grooming   10, 18, 22

Illnesses   27
Inoculations   7, 12

Kittens   6, 7, 8, 9, 10, 11, 13, 14, 16, 17, 20, 21, 24, 25

Lifetime   7
Litter box   10, 16, 18, 23, 27

Male cats   11, 12
Medicines   26, 27, 28
Milk   10, 21

Names   17
Neutering   7, 12, 13

Pedigree   8, 12
Pills   26, 28
Pregnancy   13

Scratching   17, 28
Scratching posts   18, 24
Sleep   6, 7, 29

Teeth   10, 28
Tranquilizers   26
Travel   20, 25-26
Treats   21

Veterinarians   9, 12, 13, 22, 24, 25, 26, 27, 29

Water   19, 20, 21, 25, 27

We would like to thank and acknowledge the following people for the use of their photographs and transparencies:

Cover	Hans Reinhard/Bruce Coleman Ltd
Title Page	Hans Reinhard/Bruce Coleman Ltd
P. 6/7	Jane Burton/Bruce Coleman Ltd Hans Reinhard/Bruce Coleman Ltd
P. 8/9	Hans Reinhard/Bruce Coleman Ltd
P. 10/11/12	Jane Burton/Bruce Coleman Ltd
P. 12/13	Clive D Woodley/Bruce Coleman Ltd Marc Henrie ASC
P. 14	Jane Burton/Bruce Coleman Ltd
P. 15	Hans Reinhard/Bruce Coleman Ltd
P. 16/17/18	Ian Beames/Ardea London Ltd Sally Anne Thompson/Animal Photography Ltd Hans Reinhard/Bruce Coleman Ltd
P. 19/20/21	Hans Reinhard/Bruce Coleman Ltd Jane Burton/Bruce Coleman Ltd Sally Anne Thompson/Animal Photography Ltd
P. 22/23/24	Sally Anne Thompson/RSPCA
P. 25/26	Marc Henrie ASC Ardea London Ltd
P. 27/28	Sally Anne Thompson /Animal Photography Ltd Spectrum Colour Library
P. 29	Hans Reinhard/Bruce Coleman Ltd

FRANKLIN PUBLIC LIBRARY
FRANKLIN, PA 16323

J 636.8

JAMESON, PAM

22 AUG 2002
83970

Cats

Franklin Public Library
Franklin, Penn.

RULES

1. Books may be kept two weeks and may be renewed once for the same period.

2. A fine of 10 cents a day will be charged on each book which is not returned according to the above rule. No book will be issued to any person incurring such a fine until it has been paid.

3. All injuries to books beyond reasonable wear and all losses shall be made good to the satisfaction of the Librarian.

4. Each borrower is held responsible for all books drawn on his card and for all fines accruing on the same.

DEMCO